CYBERBULLYING

CYBERBULLYING

ACTIVITIES TO HELP CHILDREN AND TEENS TO STAY SAFE IN A TEXTING, TWITTERING, SOCIAL NETWORKING WORLD

Vanessa Rogers

Jessica Kingsley Publishers
London and Philadelphia

First published in 2010
by Jessica Kingsley Publishers
116 Pentonville Road
London N1 9JB, UK
and
400 Market Street, Suite 400
Philadelphia, PA 19106, USA

www.jkp.com

Library of Congress Cataloging in Publication Data
Rogers, Vanessa.
  Cyberbullying : activities to help children and teens to stay safe in a texting, twittering, social networking world / Vanessa Rogers.
    p. cm.
  ISBN 978-1-84905-105-7 (alk. paper)
 1. Cyberbullying. 2. Internet and teenagers--Psychological aspects. 3. Social networks. I. Title.
  HV6773.R64 2010
  302.3'4--dc22

                         2009048748s

British Library Cataloguing in Publication Data
A CIP catalogue record for this book is available from the British Library

ISBN 978 1 84905 105 7

Printed and bound in the United States by
Thomson-Shore, 7300 Joy Road, Dexter, MI 48130

CONTENTS

Activities

Reviews

Useful Websites   128

INTRODUCTION

The vast majority of children and young people are computer literate and own mobile phones, providing them with almost unlimited access to information and the ability to keep in touch around the globe. Whether at home or in school, libraries or in Internet cafés, young people can utilize a vast range of digital communication tools to share experiences and keep in touch in a way that previous generations could only imagine.

However, there is a darker side to this shiny new digital world, defined as 'cyberbullying'. This is when technology is misused to threaten, harass, humiliate or embarrass victims.

As access to digital communication grows, methods of cyberbullying have become more sophisticated. From nuisance phone calls to bogus websites, the victims of cyberbullies can be targeted with little effort and minimal cost to the bully, leading to widespread concerns about how children and young people can stay safe in a texting, twittering and social networking world.

How to use this book

This book sets out to help children and young people to be safe and stay healthy, to raise awareness about online safety, provide opportunities to help them understand cyberbullying, and define clear boundaries to online behaviour.

Suitable for parents of children and teens at home, or adults working with young people in youth clubs or school, all the advice and ideas in this book are designed to be inclusive, or easily adapted to meet the individual needs of each child. Some of the activities can be used with groups of around 8 to 15 children and young people, but can be altered to facilitate larger numbers or scaled down for you to explore digital safety with just one child.

No expert technological knowledge is required of you to be able to do these activities. They work on the basis of developing skills, attitudes and learning. This means that they encourage young people to reflect on their values and attitudes to cyberbullying and build personal skills that enable them to be assertive and develop resilience. It is hoped that this will enable them to make healthy, positive choices. Alongside this, factual information is offered in the following section, and sources of additional information are signposted at the end of the book.

The main part of the book is split into three sections: 'Warm Ups', which can be used to introduce the topic and spark interest, 'Activities', which explores issues in more depth, and 'Reviews', which enables you to consider what has been learnt. For teachers and youth workers, opportunities for recorded outcomes are indicated.

The book is written to be as flexible as possible – parents can dip in and out of the exercises to increase their own knowledge and so help their children, and teachers or youth workers can use the session plans as stand-alone modules or together to build a wider curriculum.

Timings, which feature at the start of each activity, are offered as a guide, but these will need to be amended depending on the group size and ability – the larger the group the longer the activity will take!

UNDERSTANDING CYBERBULLYING

What is different about cyberbullying?

We have probably all heard the old adage about sticks and stones, the message being that words can never hurt you. But just how true is this? While it is certainly true that physical bullying is unacceptable behaviour, cyberbullying can be just as frightening, leaving behind emotional rather than physical scars.

Cyberbullying is different from face-to-face bullying because the bullies can keep a distance between themselves and their victims. This affords the bully a level of anonymity and a perceived sense of security that convinces them they won't get caught. It also makes it easier to 'forget' what they've done and, as they don't see the harm caused, any feelings of guilt or empathy are minimized. Not knowing the identity of the bully can make the victim distrustful of many people.

The enormity of the online world means that one image sent via an Internet chatroom can be viewed literally millions of times around the world in a very short time, and electronically forwarded content is hard to control. It may be a single incident for the perpetrator, but can have multiple impact as it is passed around.

However, it is worth mentioning that, while some cyberbullying is obviously deliberate, some incidents do start as a 'joke'. For example, derogatory remarks passed between friends that then circulate outside the intended group can lead to embarrassment or hurt. Such incidents often leave the perpetrators surprised at the distress they have caused and horrified to be branded bullies, when in fact they have just been thoughtless.

Another major difference to 'real world' bullying is that cyberbullying can take place at any time during the 24-hour day, intruding into places previously regarded as safe. This can be responsible for a large part of the emotional damage inflicted on victims, who then feel they have no refuge, no one to trust and can never be safe anywhere.

It is also worth remembering that the young person you know may even be involved in perpetrating cyberbullying. It's just as important for cyberbullies to understand the consequences of their activities, as it is to encourage them to stop.

As well as being aware of the dangers of cyberbullying for children at home, it's also important that cyberbullying is covered by anti-bullying policies in schools and youth organizations. Within a school, the sanctions available to use against the bullies should be clearly explained, including any appeal process, and no young person should be surprised at the consequences of being found guilty of cyberbullying. Although cyberbullying is not currently a specific crime, by taking part in it young people may have broken other laws, especially if it involves physical threats. All children should be made aware of the real consequences – both to the person being bullied and to the bully themselves – if they are caught.

Finally, cyberbullying differs from other forms of bullying in that it can be intergenerational. Young people have made adults their targets, including parents, teachers and other members of the community, in a way that does not happen in the 'real' world.

Cyberbullying methods

Text messages

These usually take the form of messages that are threatening, offensive or persistent. The use of 'pay as you go' handsets makes it very hard to trace individuals and the victim may never know the identity of her or his bully.

Picture/video-clips via mobile phone cameras

Clear images can be captured and sent to others, for example uploading the pictures online or via Bluetooth, to make the victim feel threatened or embarrassed. Probably the widest publicized form of this is the misnamed 'happy slapping', where random physical assaults are filmed and then shared.

Mobile phone calls

The majority of people own a mobile phone, and the number is rising among both adults and young people. Bullies often bombard their victims with silent or persistent calls and abusive messages, or steal the phone and use it to harass others, causing the victim to appear responsible for the call.

Emails

The ease of setting up multiple email accounts makes it possible to send threatening or bullying emails, using a pseudonym or somebody else's name, with little fear or expectation of getting caught.

Chatrooms

Used with all the site security measures in place, chatrooms provide an excellent way for young people to communicate. However, if misused, they can easily become a forum for menacing or targeting people. This includes chatrooms on game sites, consoles and virtual worlds such as Second Life.

Instant messaging (IM)

It is easy to forget that, during real-time online conversations, once messages are posted they are out there in 'cyberland', with little opportunity for reflection or censorship. Arguments can descend into a barrage of menacing comments and can include groups of people ganging up on one target.

Social networking sites

These afford a quick and easy way to catch up, share photos and have fun. However, without the appropriate security settings they can also be misused to spread gossip and rumours. Peer pressure to appear popular by having large numbers of followers or friends can lead children to accept strangers as 'friends' and give access to personal information, leaving them vulnerable. It is also a simple enough process to open a fraudulent account and approach a cyber target posing as someone else. This allows the bully to enjoy anonymity while stalking their victim.

Websites

Once again, the skills developed to successfully use web technology can be misused to devastating effect. Bullies can set up defamatory blogs (web logs) or create personal websites featuring their victim. They can even set up an online polling site, using one of the many free websites offering the service for legitimate reasons, but misused to create a poll asking an unlimited number of questions about the target. Even celebrities and politicians are not immune to this.

Different forms of cyberbullying

Flaming	Online arguments using electronic messages with aggressive or abusive language
Harassment	Repeatedly sending abusive, insulting or unwanted messages
Denigration	Spreading gossip, lies or rumours about someone to damage their reputation or friendships

continues over page

Table continued

Impersonation	Pretending to be someone else and sending or posting material
Outing	Disclosing someone else's secrets or embarrassing information online without their consent
Trickery	Talking someone into revealing secrets or embarrassing information, then publishing it online
Exclusion	Intentionally excluding someone from an online group
Cyberstalking	Repeated, intense harassment and denigration that includes threats or creates significant fear

Key advice

1. Be alert to the young person seeming upset after using the Internet or their phone. This might involve subtle comments or changes in relationships with friends.

2. Consider where young people use the computer; it is harder to be aware of online behaviour if it is always behind closed doors.

3. Use parental controls on computers and keep passwords safe so that young people cannot access inappropriate sites.

4. Encourage the victims of cyberbullying to keep the evidence of any offending emails, text messages or online activity. They could help identify the bully.

5. Advise children to resist the temptation to retaliate, no matter how strong the desire to do so may be. Retaliation is likely to make things worse and could lead the victim into breaking the law.

6. Suggest that arguments from the real world should never be carried into cyberland. It is much better to resolve the problem face to face than mount an attack online.

7. Use the tools offered by the service provider, for example only allowing personal profiles to be viewed by accepted 'friends' or reporting anything received that is offensive. In addition, always be sure to turn on in-built computer security features, including parental controls to help manage online activity.

8. Users of the Internet should not accept people as 'friends' on sites like MySpace unless they know them in the real world.

9. Promote online responsibility and at all times offer the same good manners and respect online as would be expected in the real world.

10. Help young people identify someone trustworthy to talk to and ask for support should they become the victim of a cyberbully.

11. Report any online bullying in social networking sites to the service provider. Remember, they want to be known as a safe environment for people to meet, not a bullying playground.

12. Report cyberbullying: contact the relevant person at the child's school if it involves another pupil. Most organizations will have an anti-bullying policy and cyberbullying should be included in this.

13. Contact the police when serious threats are made, particularly if they include violence. Keep any evidence and get support from a trusted adult. A criminal offence may have been committed.

Finally, try to keep communication open and encourage young people to talk about the ways in which they are using the Internet and their mobile phone. Victims need the language to be able to express what has happened to them, to know that it's wrong and to be able to tell someone.

Online protocols

Young people need to be very clear about what is and isn't acceptable behaviour online, especially if they are using equipment outside the home – whether in a youth group or school.

If a number of young people are sharing a computer, one way of opening up discussions about expectations and appropriate behaviour is to devise an 'online protocol'. Similar to ground rules or group contracts, this provides clear boundaries so that everyone is clear about what is and isn't acceptable online and what will happen if any of the rules are breached.

You may also want to go through any non-negotiable rules, for example 'no eating or drinking at the computer', or explain about any restricted access to websites.

These rules should be displayed in the computer area shared with everyone who uses the computer. They will also be asked to sign up to it before they gain computer access.

Alternatively, you could take the online protocol and set the young people the task of designing a screensaver incorporating it as a reminder to all online users.

Ways to talk about cyberbullying

It is important to talk about cyberbullying with all children and young people, to raise awareness of the issue and help keep them safe. As well as teachers and youth workers, concerned parents or carers can start a dialogue about cyberbullying by asking a few simple questions that broach the subject without pressurizing young people and potentially closing down communication. Some examples are given below – and the activities that follow in this book offer further ways of helping groups of children and young people to really understand what cyberbullying is and to develop the skills they need in order to stay safe in a digital world.

- Has someone done something to upset you? If so, how?

- Is it via email, or chat, or instant message – on MySpace, or a similar site?

- Does it happen once in a while, or is it a constant problem?

- Do you get concerned that people will read what others have written about you online and think it's true?

- Have you ever been physically threatened on the Internet?

- Did you know that physical and personal threats online are a crime, just like offline threats?

- Has any offline argument also popped up online, maybe at school or when you are with your friends?

- When someone picks on you or makes fun of you online, do you usually know who the person is in real life?

- Do you know in real life everyone who you've accepted as a 'friend' on your social networking page? How do you know you can trust them?

- How can I help you to make it stop, without embarrassing you?

If you are a parent, you could adapt the exercises in the following sections to learn together with your child. For example, young people may enjoy showing off their text language knowledge by setting you the test, leading to conversations about appropriate language. If you are involved in family group meetings where several families come together, then these activities could be used in these kinds of settings.

If you are a teacher or youth worker, these activities are ideal to generate discussion in the classroom or a youth club. They can all be adapted for use with an individual child simply by removing the competition element or carrying out the discussion between yourself and the young person.

WARM UPS

DIGITAL TECHNOLOGY WARM UP

Aim

This is a group warm-up exercise to introduce the concept of cyberbullying.

You will need

- piece of paper, pen and red marker pen for each team
- prize (optional).

How to do it

Split the group into two teams. Explain that this is a team game and that the winning team will be the group that accumulates the most points throughout the game.

Hand each group a piece of paper and a pen. Now ask each team to make a list of as many different ways to communicate using digital technology that they can think of. This should include:

- text messages
- mobile phone cameras
- mobile phone calls
- emails
- chatrooms
- instant messaging (IM)
- websites.

Invite each team to count up their scores and congratulate the team with the most points. Next, hand each team a red marker pen and ask them to discuss and place a cross by any of their suggestions that they think could be used to harass, humiliate, embarrass or target someone. Invite feedback and conclude that these are all forms of cyberbullying.

CYBERBULLY BAG

Aim

To explore different types of cyberbullying and provoke discussion about why people do it.

You will need

- Post-it notes
- pens
- an opaque bag.

How to do it

In a seated circle, hand a Post-it note and a pen to each young person. Ask everyone to write down a definition of the term 'cyberbully'. If the group seem slow to start, make a few suggestions. This could be something like 'someone who stalks someone else online' or 'someone who threatens people by text' or simply 'emotional blackmail'.

Once everybody has finished, ask him or her to fold the note so no one else can see what's written on it and place it in the bag. Shake the bag so that the slips get mixed up well.

Now pass the bag back around the circle in the opposite direction. As each person takes the bag they should pull out a slip and read it.

Leave space for comments or a short discussion after each reading. Are there any duplications or similar themes? What are the different forms of bullying? Does it differ between genders? Why do people do it? When are bullies most operational?

List the different forms of cyberbullying identified for later sessions.

ONLINE ACRONYM QUIZ

Aim

This is a quick quiz-style warm up based on text and online acronyms that will help assess young people's knowledge and preferred methods of communication.

You will need

- copies of the quiz sheet; if you want to update this go to www.webopedia.com – an online dictionary and search engine you can use to find out the meanings of computer and Internet technology terms and acronyms
- pens.

How to do it

Divide the young people into twos and hand each pair a quiz and pen. Set them the challenge of correctly guessing the acronyms in the fastest time.

Allow about ten minutes for them to complete it and then go through the answers, inviting comments as you go.

Each pair gets a point for each correct answer. Lead a round of applause for the winners and then facilitate a short discussion that considers why and how online and text speak has developed. Encourage the young people to share their own favourites and more unusual examples before closing.

Online Acronym Quiz

Have a look at the online acronyms below and see how many you can guess!

1.	2L8	
2.	FOFL	
3.	ASLP	
4.	BRB	
5.	H&K	
6.	4GM	
7.	W8AM	
8.	POS	
9.	NOYB	
10.	L8R	
11.	LOL	
12.	OMG	

Online Acronym Quiz answers

1. Too late
2. Falling on the floor laughing
3. Age, sex, location, picture?
4. Be right back
5. Hugs and kisses
6. Forgive me
7. Wait a minute
8. Parent on shoulder
9. None of your business
10. Later
11. Laugh out loud
12. Oh my gosh!

CYBERBULLYING: AGREE OR DISAGREE

Aim

Use the statements to explore values, review existing practice and discuss staying safe online.

You will need

- 1 × sheet representing 'AGREE'
- 1 × sheet representing 'DISAGREE'.

How to do it

Explain to the young people that you are going to read out a series of statements and their task is to think about whether they 'AGREE' or 'DISAGREE' with what you say. Make sure you reinforce that it's okay not to know the answer or to be undecided.

Set up the room by sticking the 'AGREE' sheet on one side and 'DISAGREE' on the other. Designate an open space in between as a 'NOT SURE' zone.

Now read out the statements, inviting participants to move to the zone that best reflects their opinions. Ask the young people to explain their choices and allow discussion time between each round. Make sure you remember to ask for feedback from people in the 'NOT SURE' zone as often these responses provoke the best debates. After each short discussion ask if anyone wants to change their mind about where they are standing, and the reasons why.

Close the activity by drawing out any follow-up key issues for further work.

Agree/disagree statements

1	There will always be people who bully – it's human nature.
2	Standing by and doing nothing is as bad as being a cyberbully.
3	If young people had less access to technology there would be less cyberbullying.
4	Schools should crack down hard and ban mobiles from schools so that pupils can't use them to bully others.
5	Cyberbullying isn't as bad as physical bullying.
6	The web should be censored by the government so that no one can see offensive material.
7	If you just ignore a cyberbully they will get bored and stop.
8	Parents have a responsibility to keep their children safe while they are online.

9	Writing something in an instant message isn't as hurtful as saying the same thing to someone's face.
10	Some cyberbullying is just a joke gone wrong.
11	Passing on a chain letter that is funny isn't bullying.
12	No one tells the truth about themselves in chatrooms.
13	There are more female than male cyberbullies.
14	If someone bullies you online it is better to fight back.

ONLINE BEHAVIOUR

Aim

This explores the difference between personal values and misconceptions about what peers think. It encourages young people to challenge assumptions and express their own opinions.

You will need

- copies of the Online Behaviour exercise
- pens.

How to do it

Open with a quick discussion that introduces the idea that sometimes what people think their peers are doing is not quite the same as the reality. Give the example of how much alcohol they drink or the number of young people who use illegal drugs. Conclude that assumptions made are not always true.

Go on to suggest that this is possibly true in other areas too, including online behaviour. Hand out the pens and the Online Behaviour exercise and ask the young people to go through it, first scoring it with their own opinions and then again to show what they think their peers' opinions might be.

Allow time for everyone to finish and then bring the group together to reflect on the answers. Pull out areas for further debate, for example the young people might falsely believe that their peers think it is okay to add comments to jokes or online circulars, but actually this exercise may show that they don't. Suggest that this may be true for many things and encourage them to consider ways that they could act upon what they really think rather than acting upon what they think their friends want.

Online Behaviour

For each of the statements circle the numbers that correspond with your opinion and then again with the opinion that you think is mostly held by your peers.

1 = strongly disagree; 2 = disagree; 3 = unsure; 4 = agree; 5 = strongly agree

1. **I have a right to say whatever I like online.**

    a. Your response   1   2   3   4   5

    b. Your peers' typical response   1   2   3   4   5

2. **I should be able to see anything I want to on the web, without censor.**

    a. Your response   1   2   3   4   5

    b. Your peers' typical response   1   2   3   4   5

3. **If I take a photo that I think is funny I don't need the permission of the person in it before I post it online.**

    a. Your response   1   2   3   4   5

    b. Your peers' typical response   1   2   3   4   5

4. **What happens online is not real life, so no one can really get hurt.**

    a. Your response   1   2   3   4   5

    b. Your peers' typical response 1   2   3   4   5

5. **If someone sends me a joke I forward it, even if it is about someone I know.**

    a. Your response   1   2   3   4   5

    b. Your peers' typical response 1   2   3   4   5

6. **Arguments that start online should stay online.**

    a. Your response   1   2   3   4   5

    b. Your peers' typical response 1   2   3   4   5

ADD A FRIEND

Aim

This activity demonstrates the potential risks of accepting unknown 'friends' on social networking sites.

You will need

- a set of Add a Friend cards
- 8 × envelopes
- glue
- pen and paper.

How to do it

To prepare: copy and cut up a set of the Add a Friend cards. You will see that apart from Syd and Shazza who are telling the truth, all other potential 'friends' have false identities. This information will remain secret until the part of the activity where the envelopes are opened.

Put one True Identity slip inside each envelope and stick the corresponding Shared Profile onto the outside. Finally number the envelopes.

Divide the young people into eight groups and hand out an envelope to each group. Explain that each group has a profile on a well-known social networking site, and it is set to private. Each envelope represents an application to become their 'friend'. Their task, as a group, is to decide whether to accept each person as a 'friend' on their profile, or not. Once they have decided on the first application, they should write the number of the envelope onto their paper and a 'yes' or 'no'.

Circulate the envelopes until each group has seen every Shared Profile and made a choice.

Then, choosing a group to start the process, ask them to call out the number on the last envelope they looked at, read the Shared Profile, and then give their vote. Ask the rest of the group to see who agreed or disagreed with their decision. Then, invite a member of the group to open the envelope and read out the True Identity inside.

Support discussion all through the unmasking process; are people surprised? How many did teams get right? Why might people lie online? Would telling a lie on a profile automatically disqualify someone from being your friend? Pull out what helped or didn't help people to make their decision.

Then consider risks and guidelines for accepting someone as a friend online. Make sure you comment on the competition some young people feel to have as many 'friends' on their profile as possible. Pull out key ideas and record them.

SHARED PROFILE	TRUE IDENTITY
Name: Sunny	**Name**: Sunny
Age: 16	**Age**: 14
Location: London	**Location**: London
Interests: Love Indie boys, festivals – went to Glastonbury this year with my mates! Love having fun, sunshine and surfing.	**The facts**: Loves Indie boys, went to a local festival as parents wouldn't let her go to Glastonbury and can't surf, but would like to.

SHARED PROFILE	TRUE IDENTITY
Name: Syd	**Name**: Syd
Age: 15	**Age**: 15
Location: Washington	**Location**: Washington
Interests: Music, music, music and girls – in a band (to get girls!), write my own songs and hope to go to university if we don't get signed to a major record company first!	**The facts**: Music, music, music and girls – in a band (to get girls!), write my own songs and hope to go to university if we don't get signed to a major record company first!

SHARED PROFILE	TRUE IDENTITY
Name: Stanley	**Name**: Stanley
Age: 15	**Age**: 15
Location: Liverpool	**Location**: Liverpool
Interests: Soccer – I play and watch – Liverpool of course! R&B, cars, girls, girls, girls, cars and girls.	**The facts**: Loves football and cars, thinks R&B is okay, and is a bit unsure that he likes girls, apart from as mates, as he has a crush on one of the Liverpool players.

SHARED PROFILE	TRUE IDENTITY
Name: Shanelle	**Name**: Shanelle
Age: 16	**Age**: 16
Location: Atlanta	**Location**: Atlanta
Interests: Dancing, have entered competitions and won trophies for dancing since I was 6. I am planning to enter next year's 'I've Got a Bit of Talent' TV show as everyone tells me I'm so good.	**The facts**: She loves dancing, but has never won anything. Her mum says she should enter a TV talent contest.

SHARED PROFILE	TRUE IDENTITY
Name: Sam	**Name**: Sam
Age: 14	**Age**: 12
Location: Melbourne	**Location**: Melbourne
Interests: Online war games and social networking. See if you can be a worthy opponent for me!	**The facts**: Lied about his age so he could sign up to join the online war games he loves. Has cyber friends on all of them who he plays against regularly.

SHARED PROFILE	TRUE IDENTITY
Name: Stig	**Name**: Martin
Age: 15	**Age**: 35
Location: Manchester	**Location**: Manchester
Interests: Skating, working on a graffiti project and campaigning for more skate parks in the area. Want to hear what you think about it.	**The facts**: Left school at 16, doesn't have a job and hangs around the skateboard park at weekends.

SHARED PROFILE	TRUE IDENTITY
Name: Sally	**Name**: John
Age: 15	**Age**: 26
Location: Langholm	**Location**: Glasgow
Interests: Ballet, tap and gymnastics. Am in my school gymnastics team and my dream is to represent Scotland. See my photos and post yours!	**The facts**: Teaches at the local dance studio and keen amateur photographer.

SHARED PROFILE	TRUE IDENTITY
Name: Shazza	**Name**: Shazza
Age: 18	**Age**: 18
Location: Launceston	**Location**: Launceston
Interests: Just moved to Cornwall and know nobody! Where do you all go out? Like pubbing and clubbing and want to meet party people like me!	**The facts**: Just moved to Cornwall and know nobody! Where do you all go out? Like pubbing and clubbing and want to meet party people like me!

PASS IT ON

Aim

The aim of this activity is to demonstrate how quickly and widely information can be shared online.

You will need

- Post-it notes and pens.

How to do it

Hand out three Post-it notes to each participant and ask them to write their name and then something about themselves on each one. Stress that this should be personal but not too revealing, but at this point don't say how the information will be shared.

Now, ask the young people to share information with the person next to them, then take their partner's Post-it notes and pass them to other members of the group, without asking permission. Set a rule that there can be no communication during this process.

Repeat until information has spread throughout the group. Stop and reflect on how it felt to have people reading about you, without the opportunity to say anything or explain yourself. Suggest that this is similar to how information travels in cyberspace.

ONLINE PICTURES

Aim

To encourage young people to consider and understand the need for permission to publish pictures online.

You will need

- nothing!

How to do it

Start the session by asking the young people to tell a partner about a photo of themselves taken some time ago that they are embarrassed about now. This could be a baby photo, or a photo of themselves wearing clothes that they loved as a small child but hate or feel embarrassed about now.

Still in pairs, ask the young people to consider how they would feel if this photo was taken and pasted on to the Internet without their permission. Take it a step further and ask them to consider how they would feel if someone they knew then got hold of it and forwarded it to everyone. Finally, ask them to consider how they would feel if the online community found it so amusing that within three weeks several million people around the globe had laughed at and mocked their photo.

Point out that this has happened in real life to some people and that much hurt, anger and sadness has been caused both intentionally and unintentionally.

As a whole group facilitate a short discussion that considers:

1. appropriate/inappropriate photos to upload

2. giving and receiving permission for photos to go online.

ACTIVITIES

WHAT IS CYBERBULLYING?

Aim

This activity encourages young people to think about the different types of cyberbullying and consider the effects that it has on both the victim and the bully.

You will need

- contact numbers and leaflets for local support groups
- copies of the What is Cyberbullying? cards.

How to do it

In two groups ask the young people to read the set of cards you are handing out. Explain that both groups will have the same information on their cards.

Ask the young people to assess each of the situations outlined on the cards and as a group agree whether they depict a cyberbullying situation or not. You will need to be sensitive to any young person within the group that you suspect or know has been a victim of any bullying.

When the young people have had a chance to discuss the situations and reach agreement, bring everybody together in a large group.

Read out each of the cards and ask the two groups what they decided. Is it the same? Facilitate a discussion over each card; for example, why do they think people become bullies? Discuss protective tactics and strategies for being assertive in cyberbullying situations.

Make sure that the young people have information and contact numbers for support. Parents may want to access this support by going online to some of the websites listed in the back of the book.

I took a pretty personal picture of myself and sent it to my boyfriend – now we've split up and he has shown all his mates.	My girlfriend dumped me by text and refuses to speak to me about it.
My English teacher put me on report for something I didn't do. I found out her home phone number and plan to ring her then hang up all night.	Me and my mates have got some cards made up with a picture of a lap-dancer on and the mobile number of this girl we hate. We plan to stick them in public phone boxes all over town.
My friend nicked my phone and sent loads of dirty texts to this girl I really fancy. She thinks it's me!	I know my mum's password on Twitter and have been sending out messages as her all week!

I did something really stupid while drunk, and now this girl is threatening to send a video-clip from her phone to my boyfriend.	This girl is stalking me – she keeps calling me and sending texts all day and night.
My mates and I dare each other to do things and then video it on our phones.	My best mate is putting pressure on me to get my dad's bank passwords to get money. Others in the group have done it and I helped spend the cash they got.
I just got 'tagged' in a photo on Facebook – I hate the picture but my mate refuses to take it down.	My ex has uploaded a video of us having sex on YouTube without my permission.

I just opened an email joke that is racist — it asks me to pass it on.	I am gay, but not ready to tell my family yet. Someone has threatened to 'out' me online.
This girl at school has joined an online dating site, pretending to be 23. Now she plans to meet some of the men.	I uploaded all my holiday photos on to MySpace and now some man keeps leaving me crude messages.
I passed on an email without reading it properly and found out that it said horrible things about someone I like.	My friend keeps phoning when I am in bed and my parents get angry if they are woken up.

ONLINE COMMUNITY

Aim

This art-based activity enables young people to explore the positive and negative aspects of the Internet.

You will need

- art materials
- large sheets of paper.

How to do it

Start the session by asking the young people call out the positive and not so positive things about the Internet. For example, positive things may include access to information, music and film. Not so positive things could include things like access to unlicensed drugs, spam or cyberbullying. Some things, such as instant messaging, may end up on both lists!

Now divide the young people into groups of four or five and distribute the paper and art materials. Their task is to design a poster that depicts 'If the Internet was a community'. Encourage them to use ideas from the previous discussion and to add their own ideas as well to reflect their knowledge and experience of being online.

Facilitate gallery time, where each group presents their poster and gives a quick summary of their discussions.

Display the posters.

INTERNET SAFETY PROFILE

Aim

To highlight the need for security online and the dangers of giving out personal information.

You will need

- pens
- A6 paper (approx. 4 × 6")
- box.

How to do it

Give each young person a sheet of paper and a pen and ask them to write down their names and three statements about themselves. Two of the statements should be true, and one statement must be false. Encourage them to think of a false statement that is not too obvious to the rest of the group.

Collect the papers into the box and shake to jumble them up a bit. Invite a young person to choose a paper from the box and then read out the name and three statements.

The rest of the group should vote which statement they think is false, before the owner of the paper reveals if they guessed correctly.

Once all the papers have been read, ask the young people how easy it was to know what was truth and what was fiction. Point out that even though they could see the person they still couldn't necessarily tell.

Suggest that this is even more difficult online, especially with cyber friends that they may never have met in the real world. Online they have no way of knowing whether the person is telling the truth, even if they have been communicating with them for a long time.

Consider the differences between online and real-world relationships, reinforcing the importance of not giving out personal information to anyone. A simple guide is not to give any information that you wouldn't happily give a complete stranger you met in the street!

ONLINE STORYBOARD

Aim

This activity can be developed into a short piece of drama or a storyboard. It considers consequences of online choices and promotes safety.

You will need

- large sheets of paper and pens
- a set of the Online Storyboard cards
- envelopes.

How to do it

Divide the young people into groups of four or five. Hand each a set of the Online Storyboard cards, cut up and placed in an envelope. Explain that the task is to look through the Online

Storyboard cards and place the story in the order that they think it happened. Stress that the story is not true but is based on collective true experiences.

When they have completed this activity, facilitate a discussion about what is happening in the story, the safety issues and what they would say if the person involved was their friend who had asked their advice. One major consideration in this story is age. How likely would this friendship between a 14- and a 32-year-old be outside the online community? Would it be easier or harder to meet in the real world? Point out that the story is non-gender specific and the young person talking to James online could be a young man or woman. Consider vulnerabilities from both these perspectives.

Now hand out paper and pens. Each group should storyboard what happens next. It is up to them if they want to develop a happy ending or not.

These can be developed into short role plays or drama scenes to be worked on in later sessions. Alternatively, invite each group to feed back their ideas. Either way, make sure you reinforce the dangers of meeting people from the online community in the real world and draw up some safety guidelines, for example always taking someone with you the first time you meet, and so on.

Finally, make sure information is available in case this session raises any issues for individuals who may need further support.

It was just after my 14th birthday that I started talking to James. I was so happy!
At last I'd found someone who seemed to understand me.

In just days we got really close – he didn't act or talk like a 32-year-old man.

We went from friends to best friends – I've never had someone
who cares so much about me.

I stopped going out with my friends to stay in online with James.
Sometimes we talked all night – he was really interested in every bit of my life.

He sent me photos and I thought he looked like Johnny Depp with short hair. I sent him mine so we could look at each other when we speak.

James asked me to use the web cam so he could see my school uniform. He says I am so mature he can't imagine me at school and needed proof!

Now every night I can kiss James goodnight on the web cam.

I have argued so much today with my mum. She treats me like a kid and never listens. James agrees she is out of order and suggests that it would be really nice if we could be together all the time. He is offering to meet me in town with his car.

KEY WORDS

Aim

The aim of this game-style activity is to develop awareness of the dangers of not keeping passwords secure and open up discussions around trust.

You will need

- 8 × 'keys' for each person (4 if you have a small group)
- pens
- 2 × dice (or 4 if you have a group of 10+).

How to do it

Seat the group in a large circle and hand each participant eight paper keys. Explain that these are precious and that they should be looked after. Ask each person to write their name on all of their keys.

Now, distribute the dice as if you were dividing the circle in half. Explain that those holding the dice will be playing the person opposite them across the circle. At the shout of 'go' the players should throw the dice. The person with the highest number wins a 'key' from their opponent, and they then write their name on the back under the original owner's name. The winning player for that round then challenges another member of the group to play again. Keep the pace fast so everyone gets a go.

The aim is to hold on to as many of your own keys, while collecting as many of your opponent's keys, as you can. Any key can be exchanged if you lose the throw, so it is important to win as many as possible. Each time a key is passed on, the next player should write their name on the back.

Call 'time'; the winner is the player with the most keys. Two points are awarded for own keys and one for a captured key.

Now, suggest that each key is a password to an email account. Invite the young people to look on the back of the keys they have – how many names are there? Remind them that this all started with a single dice throw where one key was given to another player. It is rather like confiding your password to a friend or leaving it written down where others might see it, or choosing a password that is so obvious it is easy for others to guess it correctly.

Ask the group to suggest what else passwords are used for online, for example Internet shopping, social networking or to access bank details. Facilitate a discussion that considers why people might let others know or use their password. Point out that it is not about trust, but security and keeping safe online. Also mention the dangers of storing a password online in a 'key chain'.

Finally, invite some recommendations for protecting passwords and record these for future reference. For example:

1. Always use numbers and words in a password to make it harder to guess.

2. Don't use the same password for everything.

3. Don't store passwords on mobile phones, which could get stolen.

4. Don't write your password on your hand.

DEAR AUNT CYBER

Aim

To enable young people to discuss and resolve online dilemmas and issues in a way made familiar to them by the problem pages in magazines.

You will need

- copies of the Dear Aunt Cyber sheets
- A4 paper (8½ × 11")
- pens.

How to do it

Explain to the young people the aims of the sessions and divide them into smaller groups.

Hand each small group a Dear Aunt Cyber sheet, stressing that all characters and situations are fictional and certainly do not relate to anyone in the group. This should stop everyone trying to guess whose 'problem' they are really discussing!

When the young people have read their 'problem', ask them to discuss the situation and what might happen, decide if the questioner is a victim of cyberbullying, and then write a reply that will help resolve the issue.

When everyone is happy with the 'advice' the group is going to offer, bring the whole group back together to share problems and suggested solutions.

Display the Dear Aunt Cyber letters and responses to remind the young people.

Dear Aunt Cyber

I broke up with my girlfriend and she was really upset. Then she got really angry and said she would make me sorry. When I got home she kept sending me threatening instant messages telling me she hated me.

Now she texts me all the time, sometimes 50 texts a night, and I just don't know what to do. All I want is for her to stop and go away.

Warren

Dear Aunt Cyber

I am being bullied by a group of girls in my year after I got drunk at a party and did some silly things. I thought they were my friends but now they are saying I am a slag online and sending round emails about me.

They have posted really embarrassing photos of me at the party on their social networking page.

Don't tell me to tell my parents, as they can't help! I don't want them to see the photos anyway – they would be so ashamed.

What am I going to do? Everyone has seen now and thinks I am dirty.

Laura

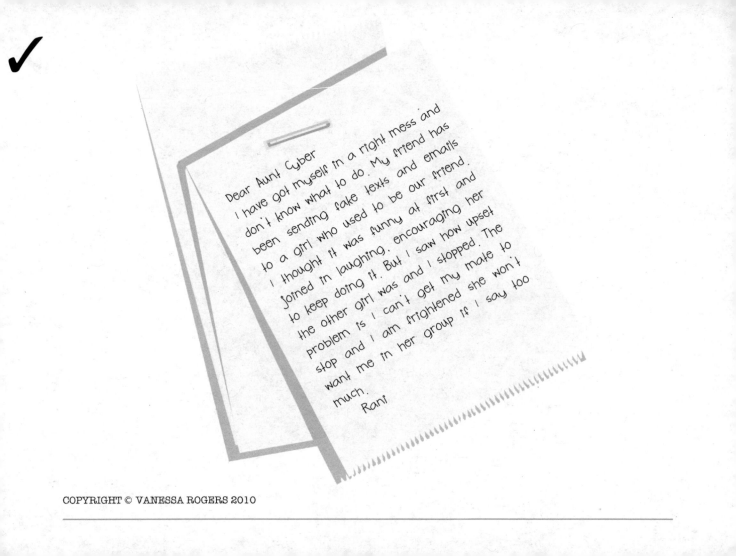

Dear Aunt Cyber
I have got myself in a right mess and
don't know what to do. My friend has
been sending fake texts and emails
to a girl who used to be our friend.
I thought it was funny at first and
joined in laughing, encouraging her
to keep doing it. But I saw how upset
the other girl was and I stopped. The
problem is I can't get my mate to
stop and I am frightened she won't
want me in her group if I say too
much.
Rani

REASONS NOT TO TELL

Aim

This is a sorting activity to promote discussion about why the victims of cyberbullying might ask for help and to reinforce the support available.

You will need

- enough sets of Reasons Not to Tell cards for the young people to work in small groups
- leaflets from any local bullying support group.

How to do it

Set the scene for the activity by saying that victims of cyberbullying often prefer to keep their unhappiness a secret. Explain that there are many reasons for this, which you are going to explore. Then, continue by stressing how important it is that anyone who is cyberbullied tells a trusted person about what is happening and gets help.

Divide the young people into fours or fives and hand each group a set of Reasons Not to Tell cards. The task is to read the cards and then rank them in order of importance, from those they believe to be the main barriers, through to those that they think aren't so likely.

When every group has finished, take a ranking for each card from each group and compare it to where other groups have placed the same card.

Encourage debate about the different reasons given and invite any suggestions the group may have as to why someone might not tell.

Sum up the session by reinforcing the need to tell someone, advising them to keep any evidence such as emails, photographs, and so on, and if it happens in school or college use the anti-bullying policy to get support. Distribute leaflets from any local support agency.

They are scared of making things worse for themselves or for other people.	They are ashamed of their own behaviour.	The thing they are being cyberbullied about is true and they don't want anyone to know, especially parents or carers.
They are scared that the cyberbully might hurt them physically.	They started the argument.	They don't know who to tell.

They are hoping that if they just ignore it, it will go away.	They feel too depressed to be able to do anything about the cyberbullying.	They think they have done something to deserve it.
They are worried that adults won't believe them or be dismissive because it 'is only words'.	They are being ganged up on by a group and are too scared to tell anyone.	They don't think that anything will change even if they do tell someone.

Source: Adapted from *Cyberbullying: Safe to Learn* (Department for Children, Schools and Families 2007)

CYBER QUIZ

Aims

This quiz is similar in style to those found in magazines, so should be familiar to young people. It asks some basic questions in a fun way and opens up discussions about safety.

You will need

- copies of the quiz and pens.

How to do it

Hand each young person a quiz to complete without consulting anyone else. Go through their answers raising the following points for discussion after each question:

1. The potential dangers of posting personal information on the web and the difficulties of retracting information that has gone online.

2. The advantages of moderated chatrooms, using security settings and the importance of being open and honest about online activity.

3. The potential dangers of opening unsolicited email, ways of reducing spam and avoiding viruses.

4. The importance of regarding chatroom contacts in the same way as strangers in the real world, and the potential for exploitation using web cams.

5. The potential vulnerability of open Facebook sites and the issues around being truthful online. The dangers of meeting up and how to reduce risk.

6. Issues of trust about photos taken and ways to block text messages and report inappropriate use to service providers and the police.

Cyber Quiz

Please look at the questions below about the Internet and mobile technology and answer as honestly as you can.

You are setting up a personal profile on the web. Do you:

    a) Use your real name and a nice photo.

    b) Use your real name but a fake photo.

    c) Post up a fake ID and a fake photo.

    d) Make up an online name but use a real photo.

You receive abusive messages from a chatroom forum. Do you:

    a) Start sending abusive messages back – they asked for it.

    b) Ignore the messages.

    c) Tell your parents or carers.

    d) Report them to the site webmaster.

You get an email attachment from an unknown email address. Do you:

a) Have a look – the subject line looks interesting.

b) Delete it immediately – you only open emails from people you know.

c) Delete if it looks suspicious.

d) Open and forward to everyone you know.

You have been chatting for weeks to someone you met online and really like. They ask you to set up your web cam so that you can kiss goodnight. Do you:

a) Think it would be fun! You fancy them, so what's the problem?

b) Never speak again – you have been warned about people like that!

c) Ask if they want you to do anything else.

d) Give them your email address.

Someone contacts you via Facebook and starts flirting with you – their picture looks hot. Do you:

a) Ask if they want to meet up – there is no way you are giving up the opportunity of being with someone this good looking!

b) Ask if they want to meet up with you and some friends in a public place.

c) Ignore them – you don't know them.

d) This would never happen as you have your Facebook profile set to only receive messages from people you know.

You get sent some text photos of you with abusive messages from an ex-boyfriend/girlfriend. Do you:

a) Delete them and forget it – you are glad you split up now.

b) Call the police, this is harassment.

c) Try to speak to them and explain how upset it has made you.

d) Speak to an adult and ask their advice.

ONLINE FRIENDS

Aim

This is a role-play activity to look at the differences between cyber and face-to-face friends. It helps to demonstrate the need for rules to ensure safety online.

You will need

- a set of the Cyber Online cards.

How to do it

Divide the young people into pairs and seat them back-to-back to simulate being online. Hand out the Cyber Online cards so that each young person has one of the character cards from a pair.

The paired cards give an online scenario. The task for the young people is to talk to their partner and role play what happens next, taking into account all the online safety information you have already discussed with them.

Make sure you stress that not all the scenarios are dangerous, but they all have potential safety issues. Allow about ten minutes and then stop for feedback. Was it easy to withhold information if it was asked for? Did you believe what the other person said?

Conclude with some benefits and drawbacks to meeting someone that you have met online. For example:

Benefits: You might make a new face-to-face friend and have a good time.

Drawbacks: You might not like one another. The other person might be very different to what you were led to expect. If you do become face-to-face friends, you may lose out on some of the benefits of anonymity. In some situations meeting a stranger could be dangerous.

Jasmine is 15 and has lots of friends at school.

Her friends know that Jasmine has diabetes but can't really understand what it feels like to have this medical condition.

Jasmine finds an online chatroom for young people with diabetes. Someone with the screen name 'Nicole' has joined the chat group, too.

After discovering that Nicole's birthday is near her own, Jasmine suggests they swap addresses so they can send birthday cards.

Nicole is 15 and struggling to cope with her recently diagnosed diabetes.

Nicole and her friends are really sporty and her social life revolves around matches and the sports social club. She is terrified that her condition will mean that she can't do this any more and that her friends will drop her.

She finds an online chatroom for young people with diabetes and starts talking to a young woman called 'Jasmine'. They discover that they are both going to be 16 next month.

Tom is 14 and really enjoys playing online fantasy games. He uses the name 'Hercules' online and plays games that involve players from all over the world.

On his favourite site he often plays against someone with the online name 'Troy' and they chat and swap game strategies.

'Troy' really reminds Tom of someone he knows in the real world. He isn't sure but he becomes convinced that he knows who it is. Determined to know the truth, he finally decides to ask Troy some questions about his life.

Jason is 16 and enjoys playing an interactive web game in which he creates his own character, 'Troy'. The game involves players from all over the world.

Sometimes, while playing, he chats with other players, usually swapping game strategies. He frequently runs into one particular player, who he recognizes by his character, 'Hercules'. Hercules plays at a similar level to him and he enjoys pitting his wits against such a skilled player.

Sophie is 17 and loves going on Facebook.

She thinks it is a great way to catch up with friends and share music. She always posts photos of herself and her mates after a night out. One lot shows them all dressed as bunny girls at Sophie's birthday party.

After adding the 'Flirting' application Sophie is excited to see that she has 26 messages from men online who think she is 'flirtable'. One in particular, 'Hanif116', catches her attention; the photo he sent is buff!

She flirts back and looks forward to a night of messaging and flirting.

Hanif is 20 and has been using the 'Flirting' application on Facebook with great success.

As he doesn't think he is very attractive he is using a photo of a young Egyptian pop singer on his profile. He can't believe his luck; all he has to do is send the photo and a few flirty messages and he can get to talk with some really good-looking girls.

Tonight, he is messaging Sophie, and from the photos on her site she looks ready for some fun. After lots of messages Hanif asks if she has a web cam so he can see more of her.

Millie is 14 and really fancies Joseph who is two years above her at school.

She is on the school intranet and is really excited when she sees that he has left her an email message. She didn't think he had even noticed her!

Millie sends a message back and feels so happy when he responds. He sounds really interested and seems to know lots about her. He must have asked around. Thrilled, Millie waits online hoping that Joseph will take it a step further and ask her out.

Laura is 14 and has an older brother called Joseph who is two years above her at school.

She overheard a girl that she doesn't like, Millie, saying how much she fancies him. Laura decides it will be really funny to send Millie messages, using her brother's school email address. When Millie sends a reply Laura laughs out loud. How can Millie be stupid enough to believe Joseph would ever look at her? Sharing the joke with her friends, Laura composes a message from 'Joseph' to ask Millie out. Hopefully Millie will fall for it and everyone can have a laugh watching Millie waiting for her non-existent 'date'!

Jenna is 15 and arguing a lot with her mum. She thinks her mum sets stupid rules that no one else has to live by.

She has been grounded for coming home late and spends time online in her bedroom instead of seeing her mates. For the last three nights she has been pouring her heart out to 'Shelley'. Shelley doesn't get on with her parents either and the girls have talked until the early hours of the morning.

After her mum nearly caught them chatting online 'Shelley' suggests that they keep their friendship a secret.

Stephen is 33 and enjoys chatting online as 'Shelley' in teenage chatrooms. He tells himself that he only wants to talk and is not really doing any harm.

Recently he has been talking to a young woman, Jenna, who seems really lonely since arguing with her mum. Stephen encourages Jenna to share her feelings and tells her he understands, as he hasn't got a very good relationship with his mother either.

They have agreed to keep their friendship a secret and Stephen looks forward to the day they can meet in the real world.

PRIVATE OR PERSONAL?

Aim

The aim of this activity is to help young people identify the difference between private and personal information and enable them to make safe choices online.

You will need

- paper and pens.

How to do it

Suggest that the Internet is a great place to learn, be entertained, explore issues and try out new ideas. However, to get access to lots of sites there is a requirement to give information. This information tends to fall into two categories – private or personal. Explain that when setting up a profile online it is a good idea to know the difference.

Now divide into small groups and ask each group to come up with two lists. One should be headed 'Private Identity Information' and the other 'Personal Identity Information'.

Private identity information should include:

- full name and address
- passwords
- National Insurance/Social Security number
- phone number
- bank details.

Personal identity information includes:

- name you wish to be called online
- age
- gender
- favourite music
- your opinion on issues.

Review the lists and discuss. Reinforce that personal information should be things that you are happy for people you don't know to view. This means that you can safely explore the Internet, chat online and get involved with groups who have similar interests, without the information you give identifying you, your family or friends.

Suggest that before giving out information online it is worth asking one question: 'Would I give this information out to a stranger in the street if they asked me?'

Conclude the session by outlining other security measures, such as only allowing visitors to see a limited profile or keeping your webchat groups exclusive to friends.

SAY WHAT YOU MEAN!

Aim

This whole group discussion enables young people to consider responsibility when sending emails or texts.

You will need

- flipchart paper and marker pens.

How to do it

Open the session by asking the young people to think of an email or text that they have sent and regretted. Invite examples and then move on to suggest that research shows that people are even more likely to send messages that they later wish they hadn't after drinking alcohol.

In 2008 Gmail engineer Jon Perlow came up with an idea to help resolve this problem. He called it Google Goggles, which made the user take an easy maths test before allowing them to send a message. If they failed the test the message would remain unsent.

Writing on a Google blog, Mr Perlow said: 'Sometimes I send messages I shouldn't send. Like the time I told a girl I had a crush on her over text message. Or the time I sent a late night email to my ex-girlfriend saying that we should get back together' (Sky News, Wednesday, 8 October 2008).

The facility is only available late at night and at the weekend, and you can check it out by going to Mail Goggles (currently in a testing phase). It can only be activated by Gmail users by clicking 'Settings' at the top of a Gmail page and then going to the 'Labs' section.

Divide the main group into two and hand each an opposing discussion point, and set them the task of formulating arguments to support that view. Distribute flipchart paper and marker pens so they can make notes.

GROUP 1	This is ridiculous! People should be taught to think a bit more carefully about the messages they send, drink less and take responsibility for their actions.
GROUP 2	This is brilliant! It will stop people upsetting each other and saying things that they don't mean when they have had a few drinks. This software should come as standard on every phone and email service.

Set up the room with half the chairs on one side and half on the other, facing each other. Invite each group to sit behind their spokesperson(s) and then in turn make their argument. Once both sides have been heard, facilitate a debate that encourages questions and challenges any claims made.

Finally, call time on the debate and explain that having heard both sides of the debate you are putting it to the vote. Each person has two votes: first for the argument that they think was presented best (this will allow for them all to vote for themselves!) and second for the argument that they support, having heard both sides.

SOCIAL NETWORKING TODAY: INTERVIEW TOMORROW

Aim

This session uses an article as a prompt for young people to consider the impact personal information they share on social network sites today can have on prospective employers.

You will need

- computer access
- paper and pens.

How to do it

Introduce the session by asking which members of the group have MySpace, Facebook or Bebo accounts. Conclude that these sites offer a great way to keep in touch, share pictures and build a personal profile that reflects your personality.

Now read out the following quote, taken from a newspaper article by David Randall and Victoria Richards in *The Independent* (Sunday, 10 February 2008).

A survey released by Viadeo said that 62 per cent of British employers now check the Facebook, MySpace or Bebo pages of some applicants, and that a quarter had rejected candidates as a result.

Working in pairs, ask the young people to go online (or do it from memory if this is not possible) and have a look at their own social network page. Using the paper and pens, they should list all the things that they think a potential employer may find attractive. Ask them to highlight anything that they think would really give them the edge over other candidates if they were applying for a job.

They should then look again and note down anything they think doesn't give such a good impression. Once again, ask for examples. What message does the information give about the person? How correct is this?

Invite feedback from the findings and discuss. Conclude by considering the rights and wrongs of employers using this method to find out about people. How does this fit with corporate equal opportunity policies? Is it an invasion of privacy or a perfectly justifiable way of finding out what someone is really like?

End by asking the young people if there is any information they will withhold now they know that some employers look.

HOW I FEEL

Aim

This activity focuses on the emotions that might be felt in cyberbullying situations and offers information about support networks.

You will need

- leaflets and information about local support
- flipchart and flipchart paper
- A6 cards – approx. 4 × 6" (paper will do)
- pens.

How to do it

Give each young person an A6 piece of card numbered 1 to 10 down the left-hand side. Explain that you will be reading a scenario for each number. Against each number they should write down how they think they would feel if this scenario happened to them. These are not all bullying situations and they may provoke more than one emotion. For example, number 9 might provoke embarrassment, but it might also produce anger. Stress that all feelings are valid and that no names are required.

Cyber situations

1. You go online and find that half your 'friends' have deleted you as a 'friend' on Facebook.

2. You join in sending threatening texts to someone you've argued with.

3. You get 5000 hits on your band's MySpace profile after a gig.

4. The person you fancy asks you out on MSN.

5. You gave your number to somebody special last night and they promised to call – you are still waiting.

6. You post your holiday pictures on Bebo and someone comments that you look fat.

7. You design a website and everyone says how good it is.

8. You see friends making fun of someone in a chatroom for getting good grades at school.

9. You have a serious wardrobe malfunction that your friend videos and Bluetooths to everyone you know.

10. Someone sets up an online poll called WE ALL HATE [your name].

Collect the anonymous cards in. Write 1 to 10 on the flipchart and write down every feeling that was mentioned against each number. If there are duplicates tally them up.

Go through these feelings with the group, reinforcing that it is okay to feel this way but it is also okay to tell someone how you are feeling. This is true for good and bad experiences.

Make sure that the young people are clear about the support available if they need it.

CYBER COURT

Before you consider this activity you need to be aware of the dynamics within the group you plan to work with. It may not be appropriate for someone who has either been a recent victim or perpetrator of cyberbullying.

Aim

This activity offers young people the opportunity to explore cyberbullying from different perspectives and consider consequences.

You will need

- a set of Cyber Court cards
- leaflets and telephone numbers for local support networks for the victims of bullying.

How to do it

This is a role-play activity to work through issues highlighted during the Cyber Court. There are no correct responses as the young people direct the role play and come up with answers. The facilitator's job is to set the scene, make sure that no one is feeling uncomfortable and that any issues raised are resolved.

Ask the group to form a circle and then read the following, changing the gender to suit your group.

This Cyber Court has come together to assess the situation and agree whether cyberbullying has taken place or not. The court will then decide what should, if anything, happen to the bully.

It is alleged by a 15-year-old young woman that two other young women have bullied her using cyber technology over the last six weeks. This has included:

1. Setting up a 'We Think [insert name] is a Slag' Facebook group.

2. Excluding her from MSN friendship groups.

3. Calling her day and night in excess of 2000 times over the alleged period of bullying.

4. Sending Bluetooth-enhanced images depicting the victim in her underwear.

5. Posting abusive comments online.

6. Setting up an online petition in an attempt to force her to leave the school the girls attend.

7. Emailing untrue allegations to both teachers and pupils.

8. Texting threats if this information was shared with teachers or parents.

This is not the first time that an incident concerning these young women has happened. In the past, physical violence has been threatened in the real world following a dispute over a boyfriend.

The young women accused say that they are not cyberbullies and that it is not their fault. They say that the other young woman does not like them and is making up these lies to get them into trouble. They are adamant that the pictures were intended as a joke and they had no idea that the Facebook group would attract so many followers.

Neither of the accused will comment on the previous allegations of spitting and threats of violence.

Hand out a character card to each member of the group. Allow ten minutes for each participant to think about the role that they are to play.

In the meantime place the chairs in a semi-circle with one chair at the front for the 'judge', one for the 'accused' and one for each 'witness'. The rest of the group will form the jury and make decisions on what happens next, based on discussion and consensus.

The facilitator then invites each character in turn to step forward and tell their story to the Cyber Court.

In role, the young people should discuss what has been said and decide whether this is a case of cyberbullying or wrongful accusations.

Finally, the Cyber Court should decide what sanctions, if any, should be imposed and what kind of reparation should be made. The Cyber Court should also consider how to bring all those concerned together and make amendments.

VICTIM	ACCUSED 1	ACCUSED 2
You have not told anyone what is happening, you feel embarrassed, ashamed and scared. These girls used to be your friends and you just wish things could go back to the way they were before.	You are angry because you don't think you have done anything wrong. It was just a joke that got a bit out of hand – what is all the fuss about?	You don't think that you should be here at all – you just went along with your friend, none of it was your idea. Everyone always blames you; it's not fair.
YOUNG PERSON – WITNESS 1	YOUNG PERSON – WITNESS 2	YOUNG PERSON – WITNESS 3
You don't think it is right that someone is being picked on, but the other girls are your friends and you don't want to fall out with them.	You feel really bad because you know what has been happening and joined in at first. You have tried to support the victim, but it has been hard to gain her trust.	You know what has happened but you are scared about what will happen to you if you say something. The other girls have made it clear that you will be next if you 'grass'.

JUDGE	PARENT OF ACCUSED 1	PARENT OF ACCUSED 2
Your role is to listen to each person and make sure that you and the jury are clear what is being said.	Your daughter has never been in trouble before. She is a nice girl who is always respectful and although you don't really know a lot about cyber technology you just don't believe she would do this. You are very defensive.	It is not just at school that your daughter is difficult. She is angry and aggressive at home too! She bullies her siblings and you have had enough. You are going through a difficult divorce and, to be honest, you don't need this.
PARENT OF ALLEGED VICTIM	**WITNESS – TEACHER**	**JURY**
You are so concerned. Your daughter does not want to go to school, go out, or do anything. She used to have lots of friends but lately has seemed very alone. She has even stopped going online and talking all night on the phone, which used to drive you mad but now makes you think something is really wrong.	You teach all those involved and are horrified to learn that your computer facilities have been misused. You have a school bullying policy and feel responsible for ensuring that your school is a safe place.	Your role is to listen to all the witnesses, the accused and the alleged victim, to weigh up all of the evidence and then make decisions about what happens next.

REVIEWS

REVIEW BOARD

Aim

To review learning and create a series of reminders to be referred to in later sessions.

You will need

- access to a computer and printer
- paper and pens.

How to do it

Divide the young people into pairs and organize access to a computer for each pair.

Tell them to open a document in PowerPoint and set up a landscape page. Set each pair the task of devising six questions about cyberbullying that they know the answers to. Then create 12 slides: six questions, followed by six answers. Print as a handout with six slides per page. The questions will be on one sheet and the answers on another.

Take the question sheet and carefully cut round three sides, leaving the top, to create a flap.

Now, place the question sheet on top of the answer sheet and glue the top edges, making sure that the top sheet doesn't get glued down anywhere else. Check by lifting the flap; you should be able to see the answers.

Finally, invite the young people to swap Review Boards. They should try to answer the questions set, checking their answers by looking underneath if they need to.

These can be displayed for other young people to see and used later as recorded outcomes to document learning.

THINK, FEEL, DO

Aim

This review encourages young people to come up with solutions to cyberbullying scenarios.

You will need

- copies of the seven scenarios
- paper and pens
- leaflets and information about local cyberbullying support.

How to do it

Divide the young people into groups of three to five. Hand each group one or two of the cyberbullying scenarios to read.

They should then divide their paper into three columns: Think, Feel and Do. After discussion they should write under the Think and Feel headings and then, under the Do heading, provide their best solution for dealing with the problem.

Invite each group to present their solution, and facilitate a short discussion after each round. The discussion papers provide recorded outcomes for the session.

Think, feel, do

1. A student shows you a website he has made about another student.

2. You get an email showing a picture of someone you know doing something silly and asking you to forward it to your friends.

3. A friend shows you a text she has received from another girl saying that she is going to make her sorry for stealing her boyfriend.

4. You are in a chatroom and your friends are gossiping about another friend who is not online.

5. Someone at school suggests emailing untrue allegations to the headteacher about a teacher to get back at them for putting the class in detention.

6. You hear online of a plan for a big fight in town – there might be knives involved.

7. Two girls wrote a song with abusive lyrics about another girl, which they plan to upload onto YouTube.

EVALUATION TAGS

Aim

To encourage young people to reflect on the learning that has taken place, and make a pledge to do one thing as a result of it.

You will need

- luggage tags (brown card; stringed ones work best)
- drawing pins/thumb tacks
- pens.

How to do it

To prepare for the activity, clear and mark off a wall space to use as a display area. Hand each young person a string luggage tag and a pen. On one side they should write their name. On the other they should think about the session they have taken part in and write down one thing that they are going to do now. This should be something achievable, for example looking on one of the anti-bullying websites listed at the end of this book to find out more, or asking to see their school or college policy.

When everyone has made their 'pledges' give out drawing pins/thumb tacks and invite them to stick the tag up in the display area. Display the tags name side up and leave them to refer back to over the next sessions to see who has kept their pledges.

As tasks are completed, take the tags down and ask young people to write about fulfilling their pledge. These can then be used as recorded outcomes of learning.

CYBER POSTERS

Aim

This activity creates a visual review of learning that can also inform other young people.

You will need

- selection of poster titles
- large sheets of paper or poster board
- a good selection of coloured marker pens.

How to do it

In advance, on small pieces of paper, write some poster titles that relate to the session you have just facilitated. Example titles for posters are:

- What is Cyberbullying?
- Who is a Cyberbully?

- Types of Cyberbullying
- Someone to Tell
- Our Cyber Policy.

Divide the young people into small groups and then explain that the task for each group is to design a poster from the title they are given. The rules for the task are:

1. Everyone should take part.

2. Each poster should have at least five important points on it.

3. Each group will present their poster.

4. Posters will be displayed to remind participants of the session and inform other young people.

Hand out a title, paper and marker pens to each group and allow 15 minutes for them to complete the task.

Invite each group to present their poster, leading a round of applause after each and encouraging questions and debate.

Display the posters where they can be seen.

USEFUL WEBSITES

These websites contain cyberbullying information and are useful for updating legislation and knowledge. However, the author can take no responsibility for the contents, and the views expressed are not necessarily shared or endorsed because they are included.

www.anti-bullyingalliance.org.uk
The Alliance brings together over 60 organizations onto one website with the aim of reducing bullying.

www.bbc.co.uk/switch/surgery/advice/your_world/bullying/bullying_are_you_a_bully
www.bbc.co.uk/switch/surgery/advice/your_world/bullying/bullying_are_you_being_bullied
Web pages from the BBC with resources and information on cyberbullying and how to combat it.

www.bullying.co.uk
Young people's website based in the UK offering information and support.

www.chatdanger.com
The site is all about the potential dangers of using interactive services, such as chat, games and email.

www.childnet.com
Advises on Internet safety and has a range of leaflets for children and parents.

www.cyberbullying.org
This is a Canadian-based site set up to advise and support young people on preventing and taking action against cyberbullying.

www.cyberbullying.us
Cyberbullying Research Center provides information about cyberbullying among adolescents. It offers fact sheets, cases, research and stories to help stop online cruelty.

www.cybermentors.org.uk
This UK website is all about young people helping and supporting each other online.

www.digizen.org
A website to support and showcase young people's positive social engagement and participation online.

www.stopcyberbullying.org
This US website has been set up by Parry Aftab, a cyberspace lawyer and child advocate. It offers support and guidance to young people and parents about how to stay safe online.

www.stoptextbully.com
An interactive website that helps young people tackle mobile phone and online bullying and prevent it ever happening to them. There's also advice for pupils, parents, carers and teachers.

www.thinkuknow.co.uk
Information from the Child Exploitation and Online Protection Centre about how to stay safe online.

www.websafecrackerz.com
A website for children and young people, focusing on cyberbullying and how to deal with phone abuse.